7 Marriage Gifts
for 7 Days
To Make
Your Good Marriage Great
or Your Bad Marriage Better

Richard W Linford

Elizabeth Barrett Browning (1806-1861)
expressed her love to her husband Robert in
the words of her poem "How do I love thee, let
me count the ways!"

How do I love thee? Let me count the ways.
I love thee to the depth and breadth and height
My soul can reach, when feeling out of sight
For the ends of Being and ideal Grace.
I love thee to the level of everyday's
Most quiet need, by sun and candle-light.
I love thee freely, as men strive for Right;
I love thee purely, as they turn from Praise.
I love thee with a passion put to use
In my old griefs, and with my childhood's faith
I love thee with a love I seemed to lose
With my lost saints, -- I love thee with the breath,
Smiles, tears, of all my life! – and, if God choose,
I shall but love thee better after death.

Here are 7 marriage gifts you can give your beloved over the next 7 days to make your good marriage great or your bad marriage better. And the primary reason your marriage will be better is because you will be better. This little exercise has nothing to do with your spouse. It is all about you. The success of this effort depends on whether you take the challenge and give something each day for the next 7 days to strengthen your marriage. After the first 7 days, if you decide to continue, four more sets of 7 – all together 5 weeks and 35 gift suggestions -- are included.

This exercise of love is all about you giving and in the process changing how you think about your wife or husband. It is not about her or him changing or giving or taking action. He or she is who he or she is and you are who you are. Each of you has strengths and weaknesses. Each of you is great in your own special way. Because you are in control of what you think and what you do, you can help your spouse achieve greater happiness if your desire is to love and serve. And this thinking doesn't take a degree in higher marriage and family counseling. It just takes a little bit of thought and giving each day for 7 days. Seven days is probably not quite enough to establish a habit, which takes 21 days, but it is a very good start. So you may want to give him or her all 35 gifts.

Keep reminding yourself that this isn't about forcing your "better half" to be something or someone he or she is not. It is not about changing your spouse. It is not about you being happy. It is all about you being more Christ-like toward your husband or wife so he or she is happy.

I once received this advice: "If anything is going wrong in your marriage, it is simply because you or your spouse is not being Christ-like."

You can't control how giving and Christ-like your spouse is. You can control how giving and Christ-like you are.

These 35 marriage gift suggestions are not in any particular order; and because they are only suggestions and I am a male, my suggestions may say more about me than you might want to know. So be it. They may even suggest that I am not highly sensitive to what women, including my wife, might want and need at any particular moment in this complex cosmos. Your spouse probably needs something different from mine. So do your best to tune in to what your spouse wants and needs. Of course, a best course of action is to ask what he or she really wants and factor those comments into your 7 day "giving" exercise.

Right now my invitation is for you to help God change you into a more Christ-like giving person. Help God change any of your self-serving selfishness into Christ's other-serving selflessness. So give it your best shot for 7 days. Do your best to give so your spouse experiences more peace and happiness.

One more time, this is not about you achieving greater happiness. This is about you giving so your husband or your wife has greater happiness.

In the giving process, so the heavenly promise goes, you will receive greater happiness. What you give will flow back to you measured as to how much and how well you give.

Said simply using words of the Savior, "Give [happiness to your spouse], and [happiness] shall be given unto you; good measure, pressed down, and shaken together, and running over, shall [your husband or wife] give into your bosom." (Luke 6:38.)

The principle is "Be Christ-like and give to your spouse." The process is "Give for 7 days and if you feel up to it 35 days." My invitation to you is to love and care for and give to your husband or wife in a Christ-like way for the next 7 to 35 days. Your Christ-like giving will change you and you will be happier and your marriage will also be better and happier.

Where given your marriage you don't think one of my daily giving suggestions makes sense, write your own in the space provided. The point is to demonstrate your love for your spouse in your best Christ-like giving way. Use each of my 7 or 35 suggestions or write your own list in the space provided.

Choose what to give on which day according to your understanding of what Jesus Christ would give in the situation and according to your ideas about what your wife or husband really wants and needs.

The important thing is to give a positive gift to your spouse daily for 7 days and if you feel up to it for 35 days.

1. **MONDAY. PRAY for your spouse.** *Other*

2. *TUESDAY. MAIL A LETTER expressing your love and thanks. Other*

3. *WEDNESDAY. SAY I LOVE YOU when you leave or come home. Other*

4. *THURSDAY. FORGIVE. Find a quiet place and say several times: "I forgive her!" or "I forgive him!"* Other

5. *FRIDAY. BREAKFAST TOGETHER. Get up early and fix a super not a superficial breakfast. Make the best. Gather the ingredients the day before. Don't wake him or her up. This is not breakfast in bed. This is super breakfast in the kitchen or dining room with best china and silverware not paper plates. This works especially if your spouse considers food to be one or his or her primary love languages.* Other

6. *SATURDAY. COMPLIMENT several times specific good things about your spouse.* Other

7. *SABBATH. GO TO CHURCH together.* Other

8. **MONDAY.** *Today,* **DO NOT CRITICIZE** *for any* **reason.** *Other*

9. **TUESDAY. EMAIL a love note.** *Other*

10. *WEDNESDAY. HAVE DELIVERED a box of candy and or flowers or a gift of your choosing with a love note attached..* Other

11. *THURSDAY. TUNE UP YOUR HYGIENE. Bathe or shower. Use mouthwash. Get rid of hair in your nose, ears and elsewhere. Put on nice clothes.* Other

12. *FRIDAY. APOLOGIZE. Obviously there needs to be a quick "I'm sorry!" whenever you offend.. Today, though, say, "I'm sorry for the times in the past I offended you. Don't be specific or you run the risk of pulling out the dirty wash and arguing."* Other

13. *SATURDAY. SPONTANEOUSLY HELP OUT -- e.g. clean the house, clean the garage, work in the yard. Ask "How can I help you most?" Pitch in and help.* Other

14. *SABBATH. GO TO CHURCH together.* Other

15. *MONDAY. HELP. Ask, "How can I help you?" This may be the greatest question you can ask your spouse – or anyone else for that matter.* Other

16. *TUESDAY. LET HER OR HIM CHOOSE WHAT THE TWO OF YOU DO DURING THE DAY. Agree that "On odd days from now on you choose what we do. On even days I will choose what we do. Or vice versa." This little agreement may solve most if not all of the contention in your marriage.* Other

17. *WEDNESDAY. MAKE EYE CONTACT AND SMILE at your spouse often.* Other

18. *THURSDAY. TOUCH your spouse. Hold hands. Kiss. Hug. You know what works.* Other

19. *FRIDAY. MUSIC. Get tickets for the symphony or a concert he or she might like. If your trust level is high enough, don't talk about whether to do this. Have the tickets in hand when you let him or her know what you have done.* Other

20. *SATURDAY. EAT OUT OR EAT IN. Fix, have delivered, or go out to a restaurant. Make it fun and special.* Other

21. *SABBATH. ATTEND CHURCH together.* Other

22. *MONDAY. WALK AND LISTEN. Go for a walk together.* Other

23. *TUESDAY. EXERCISE. Ramp up your exercise program so you are fit and look better.* Other

24. *WEDNESDAY. JETTISON ANY ADDICTION OR SIN that is troubling your relationship. (e.g. pornography if that is a problem for you) Other*

25. *THURSDAY. IF YOU HAPPEN TO BE SOMEONE WHO IS NOT ORDERLY AND TIDY, CLEAN UP your space without being asked – bedroom, office, garage. Other*

26. *FRIDAY. GIVE YOUR SPOUSE A SPECIAL GIFT. You know what he or she would appreciate.* (e.g. Jewelry, food, music, clothes, a trip) Other

27. *SATURDAY. TOGETHER CALENDAR things to do for the coming week.* Other

28. *SABBATH. PRAY TOGETHER. Pray with your spouse. Pray for your spouse. If it is your first time praying out loud, say: Our Father in Heaven, We thank thee for ?. We ask thee for ?. In the name of Jesus Christ, Amen.* Other

29. *MONDAY. CHOCOLATE OR CANDY. If he or she likes chocolate or candy, buy some light or dark chocolate or other candy your spouse likes.* Other

30. *TUESDAY. TODAY BE ESPECIALLLY COURTEOUS AND RESPECTFUL -- THOUGH YOU OUGHT TO BE COURTEOUS AND RESPECTFUL EVERY DAY,* Other

31. *WEDNESDAY. ENJOY A MOVIE OR VISIT TO THE GYM together.* Other

32. *THURSDAY. REMEMBER HUSBANDS AND WIVES ARE ALWAYS TO BE FAITHFUL TO EACH OTHER. Think about the many temptations on television, in movies, at work or otherwise. Several times today, repeat in your mind or out loud the words of the Savior: "It is written: Thou shalt love thy spouse with all thy heart." (D&C 42:23)* Other

33. *FRIDAY. RECREATE ONE OF YOUR FIRST FUN DATES. You knew what worked then. You know what works now.* Other

34. *SATURDAY. START A NIGHTLY HABIT OF READING TOGETHER. Choose a book of scripture or other good book you both will like and just before you go to sleep, take turns reading a chapter or few pages out loud. My wife and I have read hundreds of books this way to our mutual satisfaction.* Other

35. *SABBATH. HONOR THE SABBATH. TOGETHER. (Read Isaiah 58.)* Other

LOVE, SERVE, HONOR, AND FOLLOW JESUS CHRIST.

If something is not right in your marriage it is because one of you is not or both of you are not following the teachings of Jesus Christ. He is the Light and the Life of the World. He is the true source of love and happiness in your marriage. Figure out what you are doing that is contrary to the teachings of Jesus Christ and repent of those tings and give more to your spouse each day and each week and you will find greater happiness in your marriage. Other

As you give to make your spouse happy, think deeply about this quote of James Russell Lowell's from his Vision of Sir Launfal (pt. II, st. 8): "For the gift without the giver is bare; Who gives himself with his alms feeds three, -- Himself, his hungering neighbor, and me."

P.S. I work at being a good husband, dad and grandfather. I am an artist, lawyer, businessman, and writer. I am a member of The Church of Jesus Christ of Latter-day Saints (the Mormons).

My philosophy of life is to use my talents to honor God the Father and His Son Jesus Christ and to honor my family.

You can build and enjoy a great marriage but it requires effort -- 7 days, 35 days, 7 weeks, 7 months, 7 years, a lifetime.

Footnote 1. Twenty Ways to Make a Good Marriage Great

By Richard W. Linford

Richard W. Linford, "Twenty Ways to Make a Good Marriage Great," Ensign, Dec 1983, 64.

1. Night and Morning Prayer ... to say thanks, to ask for help in your marriage and family, to worship together.

2. A Weekly Planning Meeting ... to discuss the calendar, talk over needs and problems, decide priorities and next steps. (Write decisions in a journal, including goals and discussion topics, and reasons for each.)

3. A Daily Phone Call or Personal Conversation ... to say "I love you," to touch base, to discuss the day, to show you care.

4. A Weekly Date ... to a favorite park, a concert, the library, the gym; or staying home for a candlelight dinner, a game, or a mutual hobby.

5. Patience Regardless ... of missed meals, tardiness, forgotten favors, a thoughtless remark, impatience.

6. Daily Service ... helping with house or yard work, mending a piece of clothing, taking a turn with the sick baby, fixing a favorite meal. (Write it down. Do it!)

7. *A Budget* ... to tie down income and expenses, help set financial goals, and give you control over your finances.

8. *Listening* ... not only to what is said, but also to what is meant.

9. *Regular Attendance* ... at church—and where possible—the temple.

10. *Daily Scripture Reading* ... to learn the gospel, to receive inspiration for yourself and your marriage, to become more like Jesus.

11. *Working Together* ... caring for a garden, painting a bedroom, washing the car, scrubbing floors, building a piece of furniture, writing a poem together, team teaching a class.

12. *Forgiving Each Other* ... always learning from each other, trying a different way, being the first to make peace.

13. *Courtesies* ... like saying please and thank you, not interrupting or belittling, not doing all the talking, continuing the niceties of courtship.

14. *Soft and Kind Words* ... of tenderness, compassion, empathy.

15. *Learning Together by* ... reading to each other, discussing ideas, taking a class.

16. *Respecting* ... opinions, ideas, privacy.

17. *Supporting Your Spouse's* ... Church callings and righteous goals.

18. *Caring for Your Spouse's Family by* ... enjoying their company, praying for them, serving them, overlooking differences.

19. *Occasional Gifts* ... such as a note, a needed item—but mostly gifts of *time* and *self.*

20. *Loving with All Your Heart.* "Thou shalt love thy wife [thy husband] with all thy heart, and shalt cleave unto her [him] and none else." (*D&C 42:22.*)

Footnote 2
Twelve Marriage Love Languages

Take a few minutes and prioritize them for you.

1. Courtesies
2. Good food
3. Forgiveness
4. Friendship
5. Fun activities
6. Listening
7. Physical relations
8. Service together
9. Talking together
10. Time and attention
11. Touch
12. Worshipping together

Footnote 3
Marriage Love Statements

1. I promise I will keep my marriage covenant with you.
2. I will be charitable and kind to you.
3. I have confidence in you.
4. I will be courteous to you.
5. I will continue our courtship.
6. I love you.
7. I love our family.
8. I love your family.
9. I forgive you.
10. Will you forgive me?
11. You are my best friend.
12. I am committed to be gentle with you.
13. I am glad we have mutual goals.
14. How can I help you?
15. Let's worship together.
16. I see the humor in this situation.
17. I will be well groomed and careful about my hygiene.
18. I am listening to you.
19. We can work this out together.
20. Would you like to choose what we do on the odd days and I'll choose on even days.
21. I will choose a quality and improve.
22. I'm sorry.
23. I will say please.

24. I feel peaceful when we pray together.
25. I am committed to work it out.
26. I am committed to decide matters based on principle.
27. My priorities place you at the top of my list.
28. I am committed to provide for you.
29. I respect you.
30. I am committed to work at making my words gentle.
31. I love it when there is romance in our relationship.
32. I am committed to protect you and make you feel secure and safe.
33. I am committed to exercise self-control when it comes to our relationship.
34. I enjoy serving you .
35. I enjoy serving others with you.
36. Thanks.
37. I love your smile.
38. I am committed to spend the time needed to make our marriage great.

Note: Several videos on Youtube you may want to watch:
1) The original movie Johnny Lingo (parts 1-3) 80,000+ views
2) Validation – Writer/Director/Composer Kurt Kuenne 5,300,000+ views and still climbing
3) Beware of the Doghouse – 414,000+ views.
4) Return To The Doghouse – 290,000+ views.

Footnote 4
Marriage and The Church of Jesus Christ of Latter-day Saints (The Mormons)

1. I am a member of The Church of Jesus Christ of Latter-day Saints (Mormon).
2. I believe we are spirit children of God.
3. I believe we lived prior to mortality and had our same identity and personality.
4. I believe we continue to live as spirit children of God after death.
5. I believe that at some point in the future we will be resurrected.
6. I believe a couple when sealed together in a Latter-day Saint temple is sealed together as man and wife for eternity.
7. If you want to find out more about eternal marriage click on www.lds.org and www.mormon.org.

Footnote 5
Dedication

I dedicate this small work to my wife and other family members.

"Be not afraid" and "be of good cheer" are words of Jesus Christ I find especially comforting. I wish you great health, happiness, and prosperity!

Richard Linford

Footnote 6

Some Books I have written

Would Jesus Christ Do That? is the first question! What Would Jesus Do? is the second question! (Christian Conduct)

Andrew Chipman's Christmas Angel - Life after Death)

The Young Marine and The Snow (Light and Darkness)

Stop Strolling Around Naked In Your Business Empire Like "Alittle Kingly" (Business Turnaround)

The Jesus Christ Papers Volume 1: The Many Witnesses That "He Lives!" (Witnesses of Christ)

The White Unicorn Code (A novel)

These can be ordered in hardback at www.amazon.com. Type in Richard W. Linford.

Footnote 7.

Websites and a Blog you may find interesting: www.lds.org and www.mormon.org. Blog: http://jesus-isthechrist.blogspot.com/

Footnote 8.

Three Love Poems

i carry your heart with me(i carry it in

my heart)i am never without it(anywhere

i go you go, my dear; and whatever is done

by only me is your doing, my darling)

i fear no fate(for you are my fate, my sweet)i want

no world(for beautiful you are my world, my true)

and it's you are whatever a moon has always meant

and whatever a sun will always sing is you

here is the deepest secret nobody knows

(here is the root of the root and the bud of the bud

and the sky of the sky of a tree called life; which grows

higher than than the soul can hope or mind can hide) and this

is the wonder that's keeping the stars apart

i carry your heart(i carry it in my heart)

From e.e. cummings' i carry your heart with me.

O my Luve's like a red, red rose

That's newly sprung in June;

O my Luve's like the melodie

That's sweetly play'd in tune!

As fair thou art, my bonnie lass,

So deep in love am I:

And I will love thee still, my dear,

Till a' the seas gang dry:

Toll a' the seas gang dry, my dear,

And the rocks melt with the sun;

I will luve thee still my dear

When the sands of life shall run.

And fare thee weel, my only Luve,

And fare thee weel a while!

And I will come again, my Luve,

Tho' it were ten thousand mile.

Robert Burns' 1794 Scottish ballad A Red, Red Rose. The rose is romantic love and the red color is passion and danger - and "I will come again" alluding to life beyond this one.

Shall I compare thee to a summer's day?

Thou art more lovely and more temperate;

Rough winds do shake the darling buds of May,

And summer's lease hath all too short a date;

Sometimes too hot the eye of heaven shines,

And often is his gold complexion dimm'd;

And every fair from fair sometime declines,

By chance, or nature's changing course, untrimm'd;

But thy eternal summer shall not fade,

Nor lose possession of that fair thou owest;

Nor shall Death brag thou wander'st in his shade,

When in eternal lines to time thou growest;

So long as men can breathe, or eyes can see,

So long lives this, and this gives life to thee.

Shakespeare's Sonnet 18 compares his beloved to a summer's day of heat and your and beauty that shall not fade.

Footnote 9.

You can get a copy of my little book 199 Ways to Make Your Good Marriage Great or Your Bad Marriage Better at www.amazon.com. I'm working on adding it to Kindle.

Footnote 10.

The Family: A Proclamation to the World

The First Presidency and Council of the Twelve Apostles of The Church of Jesus Christ of Latter-day Saints

We, the First Presidency and the Council of the Twelve Apostles of The Church of Jesus Christ of Latter-day Saints, solemnly proclaim that marriage between a man and a woman is ordained of God and that the family is central to the Creator's plan for the eternal destiny of His children.

All human beings—male and female—are created in the image of God. Each is a beloved spirit son or daughter of heavenly parents, and, as such, each has a divine nature and destiny. Gender is an essential characteristic of individual premortal, mortal, and eternal identity and purpose.

In the premortal realm, spirit sons and daughters knew and worshiped God as their Eternal Father and accepted His plan by which His children could obtain a physical body and gain earthly experience to progress toward perfection and ultimately realize his or her divine destiny as an heir of eternal life. The divine plan of happiness enables family relationships to be perpetuated beyond the grave. Sacred ordinances and covenants available in holy temples make it possible for individuals to return to the presence of God and for families to be united eternally.

The first commandment that God gave to Adam and Eve pertained to their potential for parenthood as husband and wife. We declare that God's commandment for His children to multiply and replenish the earth remains in force. We further declare that God has commanded that the sacred powers of procreation are to be employed only between man and woman, lawfully wedded as husband and wife.

We declare the means by which mortal life is created to be divinely appointed. We affirm the sanctity of life and of its importance in God's eternal plan.

Husband and wife have a solemn responsibility to love and care for each other and for their children. "Children are an heritage of the Lord" (Psalms 127:3). Parents have a sacred duty to rear their children in love and righteousness, to provide for their physical and spiritual needs, to teach them to love and serve one another, to observe the commandments of God and to be law-abiding citizens wherever they live. Husbands and wives—mothers and fathers—will be held accountable before God for the discharge of these obligations.

The family is ordained of God. Marriage between man and woman is essential to His eternal plan. Children are entitled to birth within the bonds of matrimony, and to be reared by a father and a mother who honor marital vows with complete fidelity. Happiness in family life is most likely to be achieved when founded upon the teachings of the Lord Jesus Christ. Successful marriages and families are established and maintained on principles of faith, prayer, repentance, forgiveness, respect, love, compassion, work, and wholesome recreational activities. By divine design, fathers are to preside over their families in love and righteousness and are responsible to provide the necessities of life and protection for their families. Mothers are primarily responsible for the nurture of their children. In these sacred responsibilities, fathers and mothers are obligated to help one another as equal partners. Disability, death, or other circumstances may necessitate individual adaptation. Extended families should lend support when needed.

We warn that individuals who violate covenants of chastity, who abuse spouse or offspring, or who fail to fulfill family responsibilities will one day stand accountable before God. Further, we warn that the disintegration of the family will bring upon individuals, communities, and nations the calamities foretold by ancient and modern prophets.

We call upon responsible citizens and officers of government everywhere to promote those measures designed to maintain and strengthen the family as the fundamental unit of society.

This proclamation was read by President Gordon B. Hinckley as part of his message at the General Relief Society Meeting of The Church of Jesus Christ of Latter-day Saints which was held September 23, 1995, in Salt Lake City, Utah.

(See www.lds.org.)

7 Marriage Gifts
for 7 Days

To Make
Your Good Marriage Great
or Your Bad Marriage Better

Richard W Linford

www.ingramcontent.com/pod-product-compliance
Lightning Source LLC
Chambersburg PA
CBHW081305040426
42452CB00014B/2662